D1325917

Take a look inside my home

# Rainforest

the
**BIG**
PICTURE

**Sarah Levete**

Published 2010 by
A&C Black Publishers Ltd.
36 Soho Square, London, W1D 3QY

www.acblack.com

ISBN  HB 978-1-4081-2786-5
      PB 978-1-4081-3153-4

Text copyright © 2010 Sarah Levete

Produced for A&C Black by Calcium. www.calciumcreative.co.uk

Printed and bound in China by C&C Offset Printing Co.

**Acknowledgements**

The publishers would like to thank the following for their kind permission to reproduce their photographs:

**Cover:** Shutterstock: Tom C Amon (front), Ethylalkohol (back). **Pages:** Fotolia: Roman Shiyanov 19; Shutterstock: Galyna Andrushko 6-7, Anyka 6-7, Matthew Cole 16, Ethylalkohol 14, Frontpage 20-21, Eric Gevaert 1, 8, Eric Isselée 11, Kkaplin 9, 24, Timur Kulgarin 13, Michael Lynch 17, Steve Mann 8-9, Antonio Jorge Nunes 4-5, 16-17, Dr. Morley Read 2-3, 15, 18-19, 22-23, Rsfatt 3, Chai Kian Shin 5, Szefei 14-15, Charles Taylor 20-21, Wouter Tolenaars 10-11, Tonobalaguerf 12-13, Worldswildlifewonders 10.

# Contents

# Rainforest

**This green, leafy place is bursting with tall trees, plants, and animals.**

**Sunshine and rain**

Rainforests grow in places where there is a lot of rain and sunshine.

Hot and wet

# Gobble gobble

Some plants eat animals in rainforests. The **pitcher plant** traps animals and insects. Then it eats them!

*A pitcher plant can grow as tall as a house.*

# Lots of Rain

It is hot in the rainforest.
It rains most of the time,
but it is sunny too.

## No sun below

Rainforest trees are very tall.
Their huge leaves catch
the sun so it is dark
on the ground.

*Many rainforest animals like the rain.*

# Raining again

Raindrops fall onto rainforest leaves.
They dry in the sun, then rise back
into the air. Later, they fall back
down again as raindrops.

Drip, drop

# Living Here

Animals and plants live in every part of the rainforest, from the tree tops to bushes on the ground.

## Staying alive

The rainforest gives animals and plants food, water, and a place to live. Without these things, animals and plants die.

Monkeys live in rainforests.

**Pooh!**

## Big and smelly

Make sure you don't get too close to the raffelesia plant. It is the biggest plant in the world – and it stinks of rotten meat. Disgusting!

# Frog Forest

Frogs are everywhere in the rainforest. They jump around the forest floor, and climb up trees.

## Dark and bright

Some frogs are dark to help them hide in the trees. Others are very colourful. The frog's bright colours warn others that it is **poisonous**.

Hands off!

Poisonous skin

# Don't touch!

Poison dart frogs are **deadly**. There is enough poison in their skin to kill a big animal, such as a **jaguar**.

*This tree frog uses sticky pads on its feet to climb up trees.*

# Bird World

Lots and lots of different birds live in rainforests. They make the rainforest colourful and noisy!

## Nut cracker

The toucan likes to eat fruit and nuts. When it eats fruit, the **seeds** drop to the ground and grow into new trees.

*Bee hummingbirds fly among rainforest trees.*

Keep flapping

# Super small

The bee hummingbird is so small it can sit on the tip of a pencil. It flaps its tiny wings up to 200 times a second.

# Creepy Crawlies!

From beautiful butterflies to huge spiders, rainforests are full of creepy crawlies and insects.

## Cleaning up

Dead animals and plants lie on the rainforest ground. They are eaten by beetles and **cockroaches**.

Beautiful

# Killer bug

The assassin bug is small but deadly. It jumps on passing insects then sucks out their insides. Horrible!

*Cockroaches eat any dead animals lying around.*

# Staying Alive

It's not easy for animals in the rainforest. But they have amazing ways of staying alive.

## Sssss

If the king cobra snake is frightened, it will attack. It rises up until it is as tall as a human man – then bites!

*One bite from a king cobra can be deadly.*

# Vampires

Vampire bats drink blood to stay alive. They even drink human blood! They bite their prey, then lick its blood.

Slurp, slurp

# Special Plants

**Some of the things we use every day are made from rainforest plants.**

## Chocolate forest

Soap, bubble gum, and chocolate are just some of the things made from plants that grow in the rainforest.

*We need rainforests*

# Keeping well

People who live in rainforests make medicines from rainforest plants. Many of our medicines are made from these plants, too.

*Rainforest people know which plants are safe to use as medicines.*

19

# In Danger

**Half of the world's animals and plants live in rainforests. But people are chopping down rainforest trees for wood and to build on the land.**

## Lost forever

Every second, an area of rainforest the size of a football pitch is chopped down.

*Orangutans and other animals will die out if their rainforest trees are cut down.*

# You can help

Help to save the rainforests by:
- Telling people about the dangers to rainforests.
- Raising money for a **charity** that helps rainforests.

Save our trees

# Glossary

**charity**  group of people who try to help people, animals, or places that are in danger

**cockroaches**  beetles that feed on rubbish and rotting food

**deadly**  can kill

**jaguar**  big cat that lives in rainforests

**pitcher plant**  plant that has a jug-like part into which animals fall or crawl. Once the animal is inside, the plant eats it.

**poisonous**  makes you very ill or kills you if it gets inside your body

**seeds**  small parts of plants that can grow into a new plant

# Further Reading

## Websites

Learn more about rainforests at:
**www.zoomschool.com/subjects/rainforest**

Listen to the sounds of the rainforest at:
**www.srl.caltech.edu/personnel/krubal/rainforest/
Edit560s6/www/what.html**

Find out about rainforests around the world at:
**www.woodlands-junior.kent.sch.uk/Homework/
Grainforest.html**

## Books

*Make Your Own Rainforest* by Claire Beaton, B Small (2008).

*Rainforests (Usborne Beginners)* by
Lucy Beckett-Bowman, Usborne (2008).

# Index

24